T

GREY-HAIRED
OLD BRUMMIE

and his part in

THE DOWNFALL OF
BORIS JOHNSON

...POSSIBLY

RONSKI

Editing, design, typesetting and publishing by UK Book Publishing

www.ukbookpublishing.com

ISBN: 978-1-916572-03-4

THE GREY-HAIRED OLD BRUMMIE AND HIS PART IN THE DOWNFALL OF BORIS JOHNSON...

POSSIBLY

THE GREY-HAIRED OLD BRUMMIE AND HIS PART IN THE DOWNFALL OF BORIS JOHNSON... POSSIBLY

He liked to make stuff, mostly in wood, and, in the past, all things electronic, but in his old age he had developed an "essential tremor" in his right arm and hand which rendered activity in both these fields almost impossible. If he exercised a bit too vigorously or became angry or excited, his right hand movement took on a life of its own, flailing about in all directions; and if he was holding any sort of a vessel in his right hand it would splash its contents all over the place, which would often lead to a great deal of embarrassment, especially if occurring in public places. The frustration of his ailment led him to inflict his pain on others by the only other way possible for him…that of the written word. Of course, in the great scheme of things, he knew that his particular ailment was not particularly high on the "suffering" list; there were hundreds of more severe disabling conditions, but that still did not quell his anger with the world.

The outlet for his anger was mostly his local newspaper, but if his anger and frustration reached fever pitch on a particular issue then his local MP, the BBC and the Guardian would also be sent e-mails.

The world was suffering, he was suffering, so everyone would be told about it in no uncertain terms!

You only needed one finger of your good left hand to type out an e-mail that could let the outside world know about your anger; it was easy, but the construction of the sentences and the appropriate words to use were the great challenge.

His father had also been angry with the world, having been too young for the First World War and too old for the Second World War, he probably felt he had not done "his bit", and this coupled with the responsibility of bringing up a family during hard times and with the ignominy of The Means Test also a factor, led him to a later life shrouded in bitterness.

Our man had been born to the wife of this embittered father towards the end of the Second World War, many years apart from an elder sister and twin brothers, and as the youngest born was probably favoured that bit more by the long suffering wife.

Both mother and father had seriously struggled to bring up our man during the post-war period; life was hard and oh so cold during this time. Father did his duty by providing a little money from his work as a skilled carpenter and Mother also provided from her job as a Home Help and later as a bottle washer.

The house they lived in was a council property devoid of any insulation, and without any form of heating apart from the large black grate in the small living room and small gas fires in the front bedroom and the largest of the back bedrooms.

When young our man slept close to his parents in part of the front bedroom while his elder siblings occupied the two back bedrooms.

On cold winter nights a small paraffin heater was an additional form of heating in the front bedroom and a rag rug became an additional blanket for our young man.

Life was definitely hard and cold during those early winters; our young man often helped his father to transport coal from the local depot half a mile away through knee-high snow drifts to help keep the house warm for a couple of days or so, before another trip to the coal depot was again necessary.

Food was also minimal during these early times because of economic difficulties. Often our young man was sent to school with just a small bowlful of bread and milk in his stomach.

Anyway, back to the main story and if anyone wishes to explore our man's early life story, they can find it all in an autobiography he wrote pre-pandemic entitled "Memories of a Grey-Haired Old Brummie". At the end of this book he vows to continue airing his views by e-mail to anyone and everyone during his twilight years and this story is about stuff written in these later years.

Now let's put some flesh on the bones; our man was Ron (me) and his partner Pam, the local MP was the Right Honourable Christopher Pincher (yes, the one that helped to bring down Boris) and the local newspaper was the Tamworth Herald. It is possible that my numerous uncompromising e-mails to Pincher finally drove him over the edge and led to the incident that was the last nail in Boris's coffin…at least I liked to think so!

However, that is for much later in this book; there is a lot more stuff to get through before then.

We will start pre-pandemic and I will try to remember stuff and consult my notes about e-mails I sent to various people and the outcome of said e-mails. I must say immediately that I never got any response at all from either the Guardian or the BBC, which has always surprised me as most of my stuff tended to have a hint of the left wing about it.

The first of many e-mails was sent to the Tamworth Herald shortly after my autobiography had been published and at a time when we had had some heavy rain in the area which had led to (only) a limited amount of flooding. I was clearly trying to subtly plug my book using earlier flood predictions I had made in the Herald...pretty amateurish really...justifiably there was no response from the Herald. Here is the offending e-mail:

> About twelve or thirteen years ago I single-handedly tried to prevent the current housing development taking place along the banks of the river Anker (on the grounds of increased flood risk) and often used your newspaper as a vehicle for my protests. All that I predicted then is now coming to pass and I strongly recommend your newspaper look at my recent autobiography: "Memories of a grey-haired old Brummie" (Amazon Book website) in which several references to your newspaper are made in the later chapters.

Disgracefully I also tried to push my autobiography in the direction of Pincher...once again, not my finest hour. Here is the e-mail:

Dear Mr Pincher,

Congratulations on your new position as Housing Minister. I notice you have not replied to my previous communication urging you to read my autobiography "Memories of a grey-haired old Brummie". In the latter parts of the book it highlights my campaign of twelve years ago against the Anker Valley Housing Development on the grounds of increased flood risk to Tamworth and beyond!

When will people learn that concreting over green fields anywhere will increase the flood risks to their surroundings!

Yours

Ron S.

Not surprisingly Pincher did not reply.

To say that I never received a reply from the BBC was not correct; I did once get a reply from a Deborah in response to an e-mail I had sent to the BBC regarding my concerns about Andrew Neil's obvious climate change denying attitude. She wished to know specific details of my complaint and the following is my e-mail reply:

Dear Deborah,

I cannot be specific about the precise date that got me so incensed but I do recall that the BBC news on that day was flooded with climate change issues...it was a seriously hot topic, but Andrew on Politics Live never gave it any mention at all, clearly betraying his own personal beliefs. More recently, however, on Thursday 27th Feb. there was a court ruling on Heathrow's third runway that forced Andrew to discuss this climate change issue on Politics Live. Through gritted teeth he had to discuss something he was clearly reluctant to do, but still managed to goad a conservative MP into appealing the court's decision...but will you appeal? he kept repeating time and time again in the hope that he could spread this personal wish to government and the public beyond... more outrage from this climate change denier.

I seem to recall that it was not long after that Andrew Neil left the BBC.

Briefly, here is a short e-mail I sent to Pincher around this time:

Dear Mr Pincher,

My letters to you were absolutely nothing to do with air quality, but were to do with housing development ...I'm not sure who's dealing with your mail but they need to be severely reprimanded!!!

Yours

Ron S.

By now the coronavirus had started to take hold and here is an e-mail I sent to all and sundry (probably including Pincher) about the outbreak:

Dear Sir/Madam,

I am 75 years old, with strong "green" and "Brexit" leanings, and am now considered vulnerable as far as the coronavirus outbreak is concerned, but even an endangered species like me cannot fail to see two amazingly huge (and almost funny) chunks of irony in all of this.

Firstly, the climate-changing habits of one species that has endangered and curtailed the lives of thousands of other "wild" species, now find themselves endangered from a cold virus that mutated in one of those very "wild" species that they have been abusing and endangering for countless years!

Secondly, one of the main reasons why this country voted for Brexit was on the thorny issue of freedom of movement. The EU was adamant on this point, they were united in their belief that there should be no borders within their group of countries. However, when the first crisis occurs in the form of the coronavirus outbreak they all individually pull up their own particular drawbridges and isolate themselves from their EU neighbours...amazing, isn't it!

Yours sincerely,

Ron S.

Because my partner Pam also has environmental leanings she often gets e-mails from a Matt of 38 Degrees and although I do not have any dealings with this organization I decided to send this e-mail in the hope, once again, of promoting my book:

Dear Matt,

I am 75 years old and recently attended the Bristol Greta Thunberg protests with my particular placard:- "We don't need a Great Britain... We need a Greta Britain!" I travelled down from Tamworth by train to attend the rally with the hope of publicising my recently very green autobiography:- "Memories of a grey-haired old Brummie" without much success (I'm not extrovert enough), but the later chapters in this book echo your opinions during a period in my life over 12 years ago! The book is available from the dreaded Amazon or Waterstones but I can send you a copy at no cost to yourself if you like. Anyway that's up to you, but in any case just carry on preaching your essential messages to the rest of the world as best you can.

Ron S.

I received no reply from either Matt or his organization.

Have you noticed already how I often start my e-mails with an expression of my age…is this, do you think, to engender the sympathy of the reader to my cause?…Probably!

Here is another e-mail where I start with my age; at the beginning of the coronavirus outbreak government were debating as to whether to bring in the troops or not so here is an e-mail I sent to the BBC:

Dear Sir/Madam,

I am 75 years old so have a vested interest in all of this...but even I, after 75 years on this planet, cannot believe what I have just heard from your political commentator. He suggests that Boris Johnson is reluctant to bring in the troops on IDEOLOGICAL grounds!!!!! Is this true or is your correspondent trying to sensationalize his commentary. The very idea of an IDEOLOGICAL aspect to this disaster is quite frankly OBSCENE!!!!

Yours,

Ron S.

There was no reply from the BBC.

At the beginning of the pandemic this e-mail was sent to the Tamworth Herald:

Dear Editor,

Hope this can find its way into the Tamworth Herald:- One Fine Day

Day Four of the "Lockdown", and what a day it promised to be! The sun was shining and there was hardly any breeze, so my partner and I decided to go for a long country walk...so easy to do from our base in Tamworth. Our pensioner bodies were now fit enough for the challenge thanks to our wonderful NHS and we set off through a nearby wooded area where we had recently put up eight bird boxes and noticed, to our delight, that two of them now had tit interest. We continued through a playing field almost devoid of human life, apart from the odd dog-walker, and into a fairly large and "newish" housing estate. What an eye-opener this was, as on each driveway of each house there were one and sometimes even two stationary vehicles...what joy!...to know that these planet destroying monsters were not in use! I knew it was a sign of hardship and even misery inside those houses but being as "green" as I am it didn't seem to matter, because of the long term benefits those stationary vehicles represented. We progressed along deserted streets, over a railway bridge and into the countryside proper. There were green fields, a gently flowing river and NO distant rumble of flowing traffic, so we could now actually hear birdsong and smell those wonderful agricultural aromas. The path ahead was clear of litter and other signs of human activity and the sky was blue and amazingly free from even the slightest vapour trail ... Oh Joy Unbounded!!!

I felt so good that I told my partner that my body just wanted to run, so my partner said: "Why don't you"...so I did. After about 300 metres my oxygen intake was not sufficient to maintain my 75 year old body at the rate of running I had started out at, so I ground to a halt...but at least the mechanics were still working OK.

The long country pathway we chose took us past a closed and now completely deserted entertainment centre...there was no maintenance crew, no cleaners, not a single person in the place...really quite eerie.

Eventually, after another mile or so of progressing through beautiful countryside we found our way back onto a "main" road, but "main" it certainly wasn't! There was not a vehicle to be seen, only the occasional cyclist or dog-walker ...Oh Joy! After passing a deserted pub we got onto the towpath of a canal that would take us back to close to where we lived, and along this towpath there were NO groups of young men throwing their empty beer cans into the canal, only polite joggers and dog-walkers showing us the right amount of social distancing. We finally arrived back home tired but refreshed...the end of one fine day!

The Herald did not print this e-mail, clearly because of my joy at seeing so many stationary vehicles on driveways and the implication of possible misery for their owners...quite right too (in hindsight)... the decision not to print, that is, not the sentiment in the story.

At this time, of course, we had to suffer that buffoon in the White House and here is an e-mail I sent to the BBC in relation to some of their satirical news programmes:

Dear Sir/Madam,

I am 75 years old and for many years have watched or listened to three of the BBC's most cutting and satirical programmes, namely Have I Got News For You, The Mash Report and The Now Show. I have enjoyed the continual lampooning, mocking and ridiculing of President Chump and this Friday looked forward to more of the same. I know it's not British to kick a man while he is down but I simply cannot believe that this clown of a man did not even get the slightest of mentions on any of these programmes. Has the BBC been got at? I know these are difficult times for us all and I feel particularly vulnerable, but surely we should, at least, try and carry on as normal!

Yours,

Ron S.

I've absolutely no idea who this e-mail was sent to or even if it was ever sent but for the sake of completeness I have included it here:

Dear Sir/Madam,

I am 75 years old and in recent years have suffered two pulmonary embolism episodes…the last one occurred about three years ago and as a result I am on a daily dose of Edoxaban.

Over recent weeks on walks with my partner I have felt fit enough for a few short bursts of running (I was once, many years ago, a reasonable sprinter) and as a result I usually got a bit of a reaction in my right lung in the area of my last embolism. However, today I have failed to get the usual discomfort. My partner has suggested that this may well be the result of vastly improved air quality. Could this be the case?

Yours,

Ron S.

During lockdown Gyles Brandreth (not my favourite person) fronted a poetry competition and I decided to enter. Here is the associated e-mail:

Dear Sir/Madam,

I previously submitted a poem which, although it was written in my sixties did not see the light of day until Feb. 2020 in my autobiography, but it was very dark and was not written during the coronavirus epidemic period so I am now submitting a poem which I have just written to sum up the feelings of this 75 year old:

We didn't think it would end like this,
One unguarded moment away from the abyss,
We're dodging bullets, viral bullets.

We hoped to fade away in the bosom of our family,
Not on some strange machine in bloody Tonypandy,
We're dodging bullets, viral bullets.

We trust that the week will not end in our last breath,
So we wash our hands like Lady Macbeth,
We're dodging bullets, viral bullets.

Weekly trips to our local supermarket are done in fear,
Of picking up something evil from the surface of a can of beer,
We're dodging bullets, viral bullets.

Food brought home in our four-wheeled trolley carriage,
Spends two or three days unused and isolated in our garage,
We're dodging bullets, viral bullets.

On daily walks in our nearby countryside,
We make absolutely sure nobody gets near our side,
We're dodging bullets, viral bullets.

My partner and I have plenty to thank the NHS for,
But we both hope not to see them any more,
We're still dodging bullets, viral bullets.

It got absolutely nowhere!

During the pandemic Richard Branson had the effrontery to try and scrounge money from the taxpayer to keep his airline afloat. This incensed me so much that I e-mailed Pincher, and my anger was so strong that I forgot to actually mention the name Richard Branson in the correspondence:

Dear Mr Pincher,

I cannot believe this man!!!!!

This gentleman and knight of the realm, who according to Wikipedia has amassed a personal fortune of $4.400 billion USD has the disgusting AND OBSCENE bottle to ask our government in this time of severe crisis for a bailout of £500m to save one of his companies!!!!! IF YOUR GOVERNMENT STANDS FOR THIS NONSENSE I WILL PERSONALLY

PARADE UP AND DOWN GEORGE STREET CONTINUOUSLY WITH MY PLACARD EXPOSING YOU AS BEING COMPLICIT IN THIS OUTRAGE!!!

Yours completely outraged,

Ron S.

The next e-mail would have been sent to the usual outlets and engendered no response from anyone:

Dear Sir/Madam,

Those advocates of getting back to "normal" as quickly as possible after the effects of coronavirus have eased a bit simply don't get it! They want to continue the "normal" relentless progress to global warming oblivion. Proceeding back to a "normal" lifestyle will result in the not too distant future in global famine, mass migration and huge social disorder affecting hundreds of millions of people and will make this time of Covid 19 look like a stroll in the park! For goodness sake someone get a grip and remove the old order and get real...we need an expansion of the solar power industries, an emphasis on wind power, tidal power and hydro-electric storage of energy worldwide!

Yours,

Ron S.

Here is another poem sent to the poetry competition organizers that failed to get any response:

Dear Sir/Madam,

This is an additional poem I have written during this coronavirus lockdown. I am 75 years old and my details follow this poem:

Our frantic haste to get back to "normality",
Sounds to me like total and complete insanity,
"Normality" means the premature demise of the poor Chimpanzee,
And ninety-five other major species as well as the ancient Manatee.

Where are we going after this viral warning,
Please no more along this path of Global Warming,
Surely after this... our darkest hour,
We need to turn to wind, wave and solar power!

This Global outbreak has started to clear the air,
And allowed us to get off this crazy road to nowhere,
Let's not waste this timely golden opportunity,
And give our children a more stable climate in perpetuity.

Our much-abused Natural World has forced us to make a choice,
Do we have the guts and the intelligence to heed its advice,
Some of the choices may have to be exceedingly cruel,
But for future generations, please, please a lot less fossil fuel!

In May of 2020 one Sunday evening Boris broadcast to the nation on an easing down of pandemic restrictions and I e-mailed to the Tamworth Herald the following:

Dear Sir/Madam,

My partner and I often walk through a nearby well-established housing estate on our morning walks, and before the coronavirus epidemic started we would see perhaps a total of half a dozen or so vehicles on driveways throughout the whole estate. During the initial stages of lockdown every driveway of every house had at least one car and often two on it...there were literally several hundred stationary vehicles on the estate. So I was interested to know what the effect of Boris's Sunday speech had on the numbers of vehicles we saw parked up on this estate. Our Monday morning walk showed very little difference from previous days of the pandemic, there were still hundreds of stationary vehicles...clearly on this estate, at least, people were putting Health before Wealth!

Yours,

Ron S.

I cannot remember whether this was ever printed in the paper; probably not.

Then, of course, we had the Dominic Cummings affair, with his speech in the garden of number 10. Here was my e-mailed response to Pincher:

Dear Mr Pincher,

Having listened to Dominic Cummings yesterday, his excuses for his behaviour during the lockdown period seemed fairly reasonable until the nonsense about his trip to Barnard Castle and back on his wife's birthday...this totally lacked all credibility, and any sympathy he had accrued early on quickly dissolved away. I assume the Prime Minister was given the same story during his long interview with the man and it reflects badly on the PM that he could not see through this "load of old tosh"! I believe Cummings should be sacked immediately if the Prime Minister is to retain any sort of respect from the general public.

Yours,

Ron S.

Cummings was indeed, eventually, sacked.

I did receive a two-page, comprehensive reply from Pincher on this subject but, unfortunately, I am legally not allowed to print it here unless Pincher gives his permission ...and that is never going to happen. I can say that it was all fairly standard politician speak.

The following is a more "domestic" e-mail I sent to Pincher during the summer of 2020:

Dear Mr Pincher,

I have written to you before on many occasions, mostly on political, housing and environmental issues and you have sometimes done me the courtesy of replying, but this e-mail really does need your serious attention! I and my partner, Pam, are members of "Friends of Warwickshire Moor" and during lockdown we have quietly been doing litter picks around the site and beyond. In recent hot days we have had an increasingly heavier payload of litter culminating in this morning's absolute avalanche of rubbish. We collected three large bags of waste from the banks of the Anker adjacent to a field whose owner has done a wonderful job of creating an attractive grassland area. The owner and his wife confronted 40 to 50 young people yesterday afternoon on the site and received a load of vitriol and abuse; they informed the police who did absolutely nothing about the situation... they are totally and completely useless! What my partner and I found during our litter pick was countless beer bottles and beer cans, about 40 spent gas canisters of nitrous oxide, and numerous empty small plastic bags that would have contained more serious drugs together with the rest of the more usual rubbish. The owners of the field said there was absolutely no social distancing between the mob and asked us to leave the rubbish as a deterrent to a future invasion..."let them wallow in their own crap" ...unfortunately I could not do this because all this debris would eventually end up in the river and then in the sea. The thought of more of the same during a long hot summer is totally unacceptable and as the field owner's wife suggested may even end up in a possible drowning at this site and, of course there will be the continuing and relentless spread of Covid 19.

Now to get more political: it is clear that these young people respect absolutely nothing and no-one...not even the law and escape from reality by the use of drink and drugs. If you analyse the reason why they have no respect for the law and the lawmakers, it is surely the inconsistencies and downright hypocrisy they see amongst our present-day politicians!

Yours,

Ron S.

On this particular "domestic" I had no reply from Pincher.

In appreciation of the efforts made by people in our NHS I made a wooden notice with raised wooden lettering that I painted in various colours and planted this plaque in the middle of my wildflower patch on the Moor; unfortunately this quickly led to an e-mail sent to our local council and Pincher:

Dear Editor,

I put up the wildflower area sign on part of Warwickshire Moor (shown above) yesterday and knowing the quality of life we have in our area I hid an attached rape alarm to the sign. IT LASTED ONE DAY before the local "gentlemen" attempted to steal/ vandalize this sign. It triggered the alarm and the cowardly little "darlings" legged it. I am 75 years old and lost faith in the human race years ago and this episode reinforces my beliefs! This area of the Moor is continually being vandalized and the police are totally useless...they have been told countless times

20

about the misdemeanours that take place in this area and it is in an area that could be easily surveilled by a remote camera ...but they do absolutely nothing! No wonder these young ****** have no respect for the police or even the NHS!

Yours,

R.A.S.

This e-mail was printed in the Herald and even got a response from Pincher.

Pincher expressed his sympathy and said that he had raised the issue with the local council and police to see what could be done to increase patrols in this area. He also suggested that now Covid restrictions were easing, maybe some of these young people causing these problems could have their attentions turned more to sport and activity groups now that they were now becoming easier to access.

The area of Warwickshire Moor that our group look after now actually belongs to our local council, hence my next e-mail was addressed to them:

Dear Sir/Madam,

I am a member of Friends of Warwickshire Moor and often do litter picks around the Moor.

Recently a neighbouring property to the north of the Moor has been having serous problems with trespass and littering on his property. The people responsible for the trespass and serious littering have gained access to his land via our Moor. In order to prevent this access to his land a large amount of prickly branches have been thrown over into an adjoining dried-up culvert and there is a constant and regular amount of litter appearing amongst these prickly branches. I leave it to your imagination where this litter is coming from. The problem is that the trespassers still walk over these branches and squash and compress the litter amongst these branches, making it difficult to extract. I had words with the owner of the land this morning and showed him the scratches on my arms that had ensued from the litter extraction and he said "just leave it" and "it will stop them coming across". Clearly he was happy for all the accumulated litter, during a spell of heavy rain, to be washed into the river Anker...I am not!...and am asking you to please do something about this problem.

Thank You,

Ron S.

As far as I am aware nothing was ever done about this problem; to this day access to our neighbour's land is still easy from the northern part of the Moor.

One extremely hot summer's Saturday night during lockdown our sleep was disrupted and, in my case, even curtailed by "goings on" outside. This led to the following pathetic attempt at "satire" in this e-mail, which I think was never sent:

Dear Sir/Madam,

I am a Tamworth resident in the Bolehall area, and after a sleepless night I have written this:

Why can't my property on M. Road and an adjoining property just around the corner in a little side-road invite dozens of our friends into our back gardens?...after all an ENGLISHMAN'S home is his castle...and why can't we start our noisy rantings, music and drinking early on Saturday evening and finish at daybreak the following Sunday morning?...after all an ENGLISHMAN'S home is his castle...and why can't we enjoy a bit of happiness amongst ourselves and maybe a bit of COVID 19 as well?...after all an ENGLISHMAN'S home is his castle...and why can't we force many of our neighbours into closing their bedroom windows to keep out our noise on one of the hottest nights of the year?...after all an ENGLISHMAN'S home is his castle and, of course, we don't give a ****! ...and why, when we are lying on a hospital bed struggling to breathe, can't we get the attention we need?...after all we are ENGLISH!

Next, another e-mail to the council:

Dear Sir/ Madam,

My name is Mr S. and a week or so ago I got in touch with you about a problem we (Friends of Warwickshire Moor) have with a fence on the northern side of the Moor and you said that you would get back to us on this issue...nothing seems to have happened ...however, this letter is more to do with the re-occurring vandalism to our boardwalk. We have in the past had several of the cross-pieces (plastic planks) smashed deliberately and you have replaced them when necessary; however, someone has now decided to push a spike through about 13 of these cross-pieces rendering them a potential hazard and my fear is this may be the start of a regular pattern of vandalism by these loonies. Can I make a suggestion that notices be put up that "due to increased vandalism this area is now under CCTV Surveillance" as a deterrent to these ********. Of course, the 13 planks now need to be replaced, as the council is liable to have a bill from some irate dog owner for his dog's broken leg.

Yours sincerely,

Ron S.

Weeks later a member of the council did come along and fill these spike holes with a filler that have, unfortunately, not really stood the test of time.

Yet another follow-up e-mail to the council:

Dear Emily,

I sent the e-mail on boardwalk vandalism to you some time ago and another one prior to that on a problem with our fencing on the north side of the moor; I also contacted my MP on a vandalized NHS sign that I had put up in front of a wildflower area on the site. Mr Pincher wrote back to say he was going to try and get something done about these local problems...but a recent incident concerning a vandalized noticeboard and another concerning "spiked" boardwalk planks tells me little has changed.

Yours,

R.A.S.

I may be wrong, but towards the end of 2020 or the beginning of 2021 the results of the King Lear Poetry Prize were announced and because I had not even got a mention, I sent this embittered response to my usual outlets:

Dear Sir/Madam,

The following poem (extracted from my recently published autobiography) was entered for the King Lear Poetry Prize as my 75 years of age qualified me for the competition. No surprise really that the establishment luvvies that comprised the poetry prize judges didn't like this dose of reality and gave it the thumbs down:

The Insanity Of Humanity

Daily, The Media moulds the young vulnerable brains,
With yet more and more anthropocentric refrains,
While the planet simply complains and complains,
About the avalanche of cars, trucks and planes.

Politicians promise the Earth,
Without knowing the Earth,

While other species fail to rebirth,
Amidst human laughter, satire and mirth.

Religious leaders promise eternal life,
Through the rubble and the strife,
Parasitically plunging a twisted blade,
Into the heart that reason made.

Planners concrete over...for financial gain,
The green that absorbs the heavier rain,
Runoff swells the swollen main,
And homes (and the sea) become a cesspit's drain.

The "Privileged" press for continual growing,
To keep their oily black finances flowing,
Polar caps retreat from snowing and snowing,
And white bears' hearts start slowing and slowing.

Those myopic advocates of continual growth,
Care nothing for child and grandchild both,
Care nothing for all of nature that feeds us,
And should go to hell or more appropriately the US...eh!

Ronski

My response was, probably, totally out of order!

The following e-mail, having had four Covid inoculations since that time, shows a high degree of hypocrisy on my part:

Dear Sir/Madam,

I am 75 years old and my partner is 78 years old, so you would think that I would be one of the first to applaud the unveiling of a coronavirus vaccine. WRONG! Why? You see I ACTUALLY care about my grandchildren. What the release of this vaccine will do is to allow this self-indulgent generation to get back to their old disgusting habits of pumping out huge quantities of CO_2 into the atmosphere (much to the delight of the establishment "fat-cats")!

The fact that there was no end of e-mail signature suggests that maybe it was never sent.

At about this time the Earthshot Project was unveiled and it was quickly quite clear I would need a sponsor for my rather simplistic idea (that, in hindsight, was not well thought-through) so I tried the supermarket Aldi. Here is what was sent to their customer service department:

Dear Sir/Madam,

David Attenborough and others have launched the Earthshot project and say they are interested in ideas to help the environment; however, there is no mechanism for us mere mortals to actually input our ideas to them; you clearly have to be someone with a bit of clout to get to them. So I thought, whilst doing my shopping around one of your stores, that your company might be the very people to approach them with my idea. The idea is concerned with tackling our never-ending problem with litter. I will detail the idea below and if you are interested in furthering my cause I (and the planet) would be extremely grateful:

My idea for dealing with the continual problem we have with litter is to give people an incentive to collect the wretched stuff.

The proposal is that every producer of stuff that is causing us problems (e.g. Plastic bottles, polystyrene fast food trays, plastic bags, tin cans etc. etc.) should be required by law to put on a bar-code label on every item they produce. This label would be a durable stick-on that even the smallest of companies could attach to their products quite easily and the information on the bar-code need only describe what it is.

When these items were discarded throughout our highways and byways (and countryside) the incentive to collect this litter is that by collecting a certain amount and passing it through a machine at the local recycling centre they would be issued a lottery-type ticket that would entitle them to a weekly or monthly draw for big cash prizes.

I thought maybe that for every 50 items they passed into the machine they would be entitled to one lottery ticket...and possibly for one hundred items they might get three lottery tickets or possibly two with a voucher that gave them a small instant prize...whatever.

Now the machine at the recycling centre that received all this litter could automatically read the bar-code as the stuff was passed into it and sort it instantly.

For those people not living near a recycling centre, there is the idea of a mobile wagon doing the same sort of thing that the machine at the recycling centre did.

Now all this stuff is possible using existing technologies; there are supermarket scanners that can instantly read bar-codes for that part of the machine that would sort stuff; there are lottery groups that know all about the issuing of draw tickets...it's all there if we choose to get it together.

Finally, the savings to us all could be enormous. There would be a greatly reduced pressure (and costs) on existing cleaning-up groups, and it would also encourage people (including the young) into the outdoors to look for this possible pathway to wealth.

Yours,

Ron S.

Basically, the girl that replied hadn't got a clue and suggested, helpfully, I continue on my own without their help.

Now here is a little message sent to the BBC and Guardian:

HIGH FLYERS?

The high flying human race has developed engine trouble and is plunging towards the Earth at a colossal speed and moments before the catastrophic impact... humanity is pre-occupied with the cold it has just caught...unbelievable...just for the record I am a 75 year old with health issues.

Clearly, this was never going to be printed or commented on, but was again just an outlet for my never-ending frustration with the human race.

In the next e-mail to both the BBC and the Guardian I express my disappointment at a couple of events, and refer to my autobiography in which I had described Western democracy as a future failed experiment. In light of the 6th January events in Washington at that time it seemed the cracks in Western democracy were certainly beginning to appear:

Dear Sir/Madam,

In two month's time I will be 76 years old and recently I have been demoralised by two acts, that for me, have proved total and complete disappointments. The first was the knighthood given to Lewis Hamilton, a man that has done more to help the promotion of the reckless carbonization of the atmosphere than any other single person (other than possibly Michael O'Leary)!

The second was Greta Thunberg's laissez-faire attitude towards flyers and her failure to roundly condemn them! I spent 12 years in the RAF and since leaving the air force over 40 years ago I have never set foot on a plane. However, that does not mean that I have anything against the RAF as reading my autobiography will show...incidentally the book also suggests that Western Democracy, in the great scheme of things, would soon become a "failed experiment"...is it starting to unravel already?

Another e-mail sent around this time to the BBC and the Guardian once again shows my disgust at human behaviour:

There is a sickness pervading this land and it is not just coronavirus. It is a sickness that manifests itself in many guises. The sports personality of the year being won by Lewis Hamilton is one indication of the deep sickness that this country is suffering from. This is a man who has spent all of his working life pumping out CO_2 into the atmosphere and in doing so has encouraged and been a role-model to the young to follow suit. Another indication of this sickness is in the studying of quiz programs on television; when contestants are asked what they would do if they won the major prize, 99% say that they would want to pump out more CO_2 into the skies with foreign travel to exotic, far-off lands. Coming out of lockdown is what the general public is crying out for...presumably so that they can once again pump out yet more CO_2 in visiting their nearest and dearest, despite the fact that they can now telephone them or even have face to face contact with them via the web. I remember years ago that my parents could only contact their parents (who lived within 10 miles of them) by the occasional letter. My parents could not afford the cost of public transport to visit them as the money was required to feed us. It sickens me to the core to see how human expectations have progressed over the years so that pumping out large quantities of CO_2 at any time is considered a human God-given absolute right!

Yours,

R.A.S.

Since I watch football on TV the following e-mail to the BBC was prompted by scenes I had watched at the end of an FA Cup game:

Dear Sir/ Madam,

What I would like to know is what the BBC think that the Football Association will do about the Chorley FC celebrations after their victory over Derby in the FA Cup. Does this club feel it is not part of the pandemic lockdown? What is even more surprising is that one of the guys celebrating was actually a teacher!

Yours,

R.A.S.

Yet another e-mail sent to all and sundry expressing some of my "pain":

Dear Sir/Madam,

I published my autobiography exactly one year ago and since I do not have "celebrity" status it has managed to sell just one dozen copies. However, the poor unfortunates that did buy a copy and actually read it will have a good idea of what I thought over fifteen years ago about politicians in general, "western democracy" and that shining light of democracy the USA. So recent events in America would come as no surprise to those who read my short manuscript, and they would certainly appreciate my intense hatred for the clown that came to power, namely Donald J. Trump! It is still quite frightening that there are lurking in that (once beautiful) country over 70 million DTs. Strangely

DTs also refers to a condition known as Delirium Tremens and is defined as a "rapid onset of confusion" usually caused by a "withdrawal from alcohol"...need I say more!

Yours,

R.A.S.

The following e-mail was sent during the earlier days of the pandemic and at that time the figures seemed to show a significant difference in the way the democratic West dealt with the problem as compared with the authoritarian regime in China. Of course, at this present time there appears to have been a total reversal in fortune, but I would maintain that this is nothing to do with politicians but more to do with Western scientists producing effective vaccines and the Chinese unable to do so, and also Chinese reluctance to use western vaccines. Anyway here is the e-mail:

Dear Sir/Madam,

The coronavirus kicked off in China over one year ago, yet when you look at the deaths/million figures for countries worldwide can someone explain to me why China is doing unbelievably better than all Western Democracies:

Country Deaths/Million of Population

China 3
USA 1,173

UK 1,222
France 1,053
Italy 1,321
Mexico 1,046
Spain 1,127
Brazil 960

Etc, etc.

Could it be that politicians in these "Western Democracies" aren't prepared to make decisions that might upset their own populations and as a result will threaten their own miserable existence! Politicians clearly feel their own livelihood is much more important than the deaths of large numbers of their own population.

Interestingly, it appears that there is now a call for all "Western Democracies" to gang up against China...unbelievable!!!

Yours,

R.A.S.

Pincher replied to this one with quite a comprehensive reply in which he basically said not to trust the figures until the pandemic is over and a full analysis can be done. He also suggested that they had not enforced incredibly heavy restrictions because the PM preferred to trust the British people to do "the right things". Surprisingly, towards the end of the letter, he also said that I should continue to look out for myself!

Now for something completely different. As I explained earlier I often watch football on TV and also have been a lifelong West Bromwich Albion fan, so this e-mail to a local Black Country newspaper was prompted by both a Sunday afternoon televised game and a change in the managership of my favourite football team:

I have been a "Baggies" supporter for over 65 years now and have at times had to endure our "boing-boing" status, but nevertheless for the most part we have always played enjoyable open and attractive football. In recent years for various reasons I have been a stay-at-home supporter and relied heavily on television to watch my team. However, there have been times when I have raised my head above the parapets to make appropriate comments on some aspect or other about the club's fortunes.

In 2017 I actually wrote to the club objecting to the appointment of Alan Pardew as manager, despite the general consensus of the football TV commentators that this was a great move. He lasted just 5 months with a win percentage of just 14%.

Well here we go again with another of the TV commentators' favourites, "Big Sam"!

Here is a man that in recent years has achieved precisely nothing and whose whole footballing philosophy relies heavily on defence with the hope of snatching the odd goal to gain victory...a philosophy that is completely and utterly alien to the West Brom style! Remember also that this was a replacement for Slaven Bilic whose last game as WBA Manager was an away 1-1 draw against Man City and who had a win percentage for the "Baggies" of 40%. How did "Big Sam" do with the return fixture against Man City at the Hawthorns?...we LOST 5-0!

I doubt if we are ever going to achieve the dizzy heights in my youth when we were under the managership of Vic Buckingham and had players like Howe, Barlow, Allen, Griffin, Robson, Kevan etc. etc., and when we thrashed Man City 9-2, but Allardyce is a seriously bitter pill to swallow.

I know you can't make a silk purse out of a sow's ear, but I would prefer to keep the ear on the pig and totally enjoy her running around the field, rather than some botched butchery of the pig by Allardyce in some vain attempt at making a silk purse out of her ear!

Anyway I have just watched my team (on television of course) grind out a draw at the Hawthorns under the managership of "Big Sam" against a poor Fulham team and there are certainly no signs for any optimism for the future there, I'm afraid. Incidentally, prior to this game I watched a game between Everton and Newcastle and was struck by a contrast in the abilities between two South American players playing there. The first was the Everton player named James or Rodriguez or whatever he wants to call himself; I have watched this player over the years and he spends more time rolling around on the turf trying to get an opponent sent off than anyone in the history of football, basically he is everything despicable in today's game. By contrast the Newcastle player called Almiron who, at present, is the finest footballer in the country, and is everything that James is not. He puts in a shift like no other, his work-rate is phenomenal, he "sees" a pass, he tackles well and also can score when given a chance. At 26 years of age why the big clubs haven't gone in for him is extraordinary!

As it transpires Allardyce proved a failure and did not stay with us for very long and Almiron has proved pivotal in Newcastle's recent successful revival. Unfortunately, I cannot gain any kudos for these acute observations as my e-mail to the local Black Country newspaper was never printed!

Back again to more political stuff. This was a general e-mail sent to the usual recipients:

I'm sick to death of slimy politicians, particularly on the left, trying to deflect the blame for the continuation of the epidemic and its consequences, away from the public and towards the government. We know that this government, along with most western "democratic" governments, were not strong enough at the start of the outbreak; however, by imposing stricter penalties on pandemic transgressors, particularly those involved in aviation deceit, the government are, at least, showing some "bottle"!

You see we have a self-indulgent population who expect to travel when and wherever they like without the slightest regard for the consequences, both as far as the pandemic is concerned, nor, more importantly, the effect it is having on the increase in global warming.

In fact in my younger days in the RAF I displayed the same scant regard for the consequences of air travel as the general population do today, but my excuse was ignorance of its effects, whereas there is nobody today who is not familiar with what it is doing to the environment every time they step on a plane.

I want air travel to be confined to the transportation of goods only until movement around the globe by air for the general public can, eventually, be done without any increase in the carbonisation of the atmosphere.

This received absolutely no replies from anyone.

There are now a few pages that are concerned with on-line gambling and my particular "grouse" with Betway so if you are not interested in this sort of stuff I would skip the next few pages.

Here is a very long e-mail that I sent to Pincher (and others) on this subject:

Dear Mr Pincher,

I have often written to you on political topics; however, this e-mail is on a somewhat more personal subject, namely on-line gambling.

I am 76 years old and have gambled most of my life (my father gambled so I suspect it is a trait that is both environmental and genetic) and consider myself to be the archetypal "responsible" gambler. You see, in my early life, the shame of scrounging money off my impoverished mother to gamble led to me being a much more "responsible" gambler for the rest of my gambling life. I have NEVER let my gambling get out of control and have NEVER been in debt to anyone due to gambling... that is the "back story", now here is the main issue.

Ever since on-line gambling started over twenty years ago I have held accounts with at least ten different on-line bookmakers, and have nearly always used their gaming option...it is, after all, the "crack cocaine" for gamblers. However, during ALL of my experiences with these different on-line companies:

(1) I have NEVER been asked or interrogated about my financial viability on joining these people.

(2) I have ALWAYS enjoyed early success on their gaming sites before the "rot" sets in...they ALL use this technique of allowing initial success to lure you into a more extravagant and reckless pattern of behaviour.

(3) I have closed my account with most of these companies because of what I consider to be unethical or underhand behaviour on their part; which leads me onto the story of my dealings with Betway, the Gambling Commission and eCOGRA.

My problem with Betway was that they "froze" and subsequently closed my account on the issue of "Responsible Gambling", which really upset me. At that time, over the previous six weeks I was in profit by over £500 and had a self-imposed daily limit of £10/day; this clearly was not a particularly profitable situation for the company so they decided to play the "Responsible Gambling" card! The fact that they did not play this card in my early days with the company when I was starting to lose (after initial success, of course) and my daily limit was £25/day seemed to have escaped them in their haste to close me down!

Anyway the dialogue with the company lasted over three months and involved the Gambling Commission, eCOGRA, and a considerable amount of obfuscation by Betway. I kept a blow by blow account of the proceedings but it is too lengthy to include here; however, when the dust settled I wrote the following to the Gambling Commission:

Dear Mr Mason,

To say that I am "gutted" by your response to my appeal to your organisation would be a total understatement. Both yourselves and eCOGRA have failed me on what appears to have been a blatant (and now successful) attempt by Betway at stopping an unprofitable account (by using "Responsible Gambling" as the excuse).

However, my small-time habit of chasing what remains in Pandora's Box does continue with an on-line company associated with the National Lottery. Clearly as a not very profitable client my latest withdrawal from this company required me to go through their verification process by sending them a copy of my 76 year old birth certificate, a copy of my passport, proof of my current address and a picture of myself! It is obvious that all these on-line companies are only really interested in their BIG players. Since when playing these games I only select the 10p and 20p options I never look down the "Big end" of the options, but it is really quite horrifying that you can opt to gamble £240 on one roll of the slot...Who are these people that wager these amounts? ...and how is this allowable under your watch?

Yours,

R.A.S.

This was their reply:

Dear Mr S,

Thank you for your follow-up response.

I must reiterate that operators are permitted to close/restrict accounts on responsible gambling grounds if they feel that the individual may be at risk of suffering gambling related harm. I can also confirm that there is currently no 'right to bet' in Great Britain. This means that operators can choose to restrict individuals from accessing their services, should they wish. Ultimately, it would be a business decision for them to make.

I would now like address your concerns regarding individuals who opt to gamble large amounts of monies on slot games. I understand that you are concerned that this is permitted.

I can confirm that all of our licensed operators must have processes in place to assess each individual consumer's affordability. This is so that they can identify all those that are at risk. It is also in place to ensure that consumers are not gambling beyond their means.

How these checks are made is a business decision so may vary between different businesses. However, we would expect to see an interaction with the consumer. An interaction can be via an e-mail, a phone call or live chat message asking if you are comfortable with your spending. These checks also often lead to requests for bank statements, wage slips and other financial documents/proof of income.

With this being said, you may be interested in knowing that we have recently announced a package of changes aimed at making online games safer. You can read more about this here.

Finally, you may also be interested to know the government are currently undertaking a review of the Gambling Act and the powers of the Gambling Commission as part of a major and wide-ranging review of gambling laws.

We would therefore suggest, if you still have concerns about the Gambling Commission and our powers, or concerns about the Gambling Act, that you raise your concerns and suggestions with your local MP. This would be the appropriate step to take to campaign for changes to legislation. You could also raise your concerns with the Department for Digital, Culture, Media and Sport (DCMS).

Your enquiry reference number is: 1-235767329

Kind regards,

Jack Turley

Contact Centre Advisor
GAMBLING COMMISSION
Victoria Square House
Victoria Square
Birmingham B2 4BP
Tel: 0121 230 6666

What deeply troubles and concerns me here is that "all of our licensed operators must have processes in place to assess each individual consumer's affordability". Clearly I, and everyone else should be interested in knowing what exactly these "processes" are; the suggestions in the following paragraph of the above reply have, in my experience, no basis in reality and suggest to me that the Gambling Commission are being somewhat self-delusional.

Finally, just a note to tell you that my recent experience with the gaming company associated with the National Lottery has come to an end as they have found a clever way of getting rid of the unwanted – they close the slots that you enjoy and have half a chance of winning on by using a "technical difficulties" notice and then totally ignoring your reminders about the problems for weeks on end!

Pincher's comprehensive "straight bat" reply suggested that it is not always easy to separate the addictive gambler from the "fun" gambler. He also suggested that operators make regular checks on their users to assess their affordability to gamble the amounts that they are indulging in. Unfortunately, he does not make it clear how these checks are done...the very point I wanted clarified! He also wrote about user identification, money laundering issues and possible government reform...but nothing that "floated my boat".

The next e-mail relates to energy used to keep cryptocurrencies and the on-line gambling industry going and was sent to the usual crew:

Dear Sir/Madam,

The stupidity of the human race never ceases to amaze me...can you believe that sections of humanity are playing Bitcoin money games on the web and are apparently consuming as much energy in doing so as the whole of the country of Denmark...are we completely insane? I am informed that there will be an even greater demand for energy as this nonsense spreads (amongst the "well-off") around the world!

I also know that large amounts of data are required to be stored regarding every transaction placed with on-line betting companies (even down to every "roll of the dice"). The amount of energy required worldwide for the storage of such gambling data, you suspect, must also be as colossal as that for Bitcoin...what the **** are we doing?

Are power stations being built to satisfy the self-indulgent needs of the affluent?

However, I do have to confess as being a user of on-line betting during the pandemic when the betting shops have been closed, so in that respect I am as guilty as the next man; so, in light of the suggested Bitcoin energy consumption figures, my gambling impulses will now have to wait until the betting shops re-open. In my defence, I have to say, I never fly, I do not own a car, I eat no meat and we have solar panels and for the past twenty years we have donated towards the schooling of Ethiopian children.

Yours,

R.A.S.

Another e-mail sent that fell on deaf ears.

Around the time of Test and Trace I wrote this e-mail; not my finest hour at trying to be an Ian Hislop:

Who Needs Guns and Knives?

Who needs guns and knives as the government has kindly informed some of us that we are now the proud possessors of invisible guns that shoot invisible (and often fatal) untraceable bullets ...what's not to like! Those rich old relatives of mine need a friendly visit from me as you never know I might suddenly inherit a wodge of cash; and that geezer from around the corner who gave me "the eye" for dropping litter on the floor will certainly get his comeuppance; and that old woman in the corner shop that refused to sell me cigarettes a few years ago will need my close attention; and that bloke that keeps "coming on" to my sister will need a salivary handshake. Not forgetting, of course, that guy in the wheelchair who keeps blocking my path as I'm walking along the pavement will also need a friendly helpful push; and our elderly coloured neighbours could do with a really nice bunch of flowers...and let's not forget my local MP who has done precisely nothing for me deserves a hand-given Christmas card!...What the hell is this government doing unleashing a few(?) of the more unstable members of society on the rest of us!...For God's sake don't those people running our lives realize that, while the vast majority of us are trying our best, there are, in reality, the hateful few that will take full advantage of this dreadful situation! How do you deal with them??

In a barrel of apples it only takes one or two rotten ones to quickly destroy the whole lot!! Test and Trace...Bah! Humbug!!

Yours,

R.A.S.

The next unusual e-mail was sent to the BBC and possibly the Guardian:

I have written to you with my views on the urgency of tackling Global Warming and also on what I think about politicians on many occasions and you have never reproduced anything I have had to say. But even at 76 I do have opinions on other issues and this particular topic is about the Eurovision Song Contest.

For weeks I have been saying to my partner that our entry for the contest is going nowhere despite the hype from Ken Bruce, the BBC and others. We all know Europe hates us in much the same way that the whole world hates America, primarily for overbearing brashness and in our case a hint of football fan thuggery thrown in! However, this plonkity-plonk song shows tired thinking from a tired music establishment in this country.

The contest itself was watched in its entirety and the standard was high. The entries from Belgium, Iceland, Lithuania and Ukraine all appealed but then we were told of a heavy metal entry from Italy. WHAT!...Can this be true? Well, this was heavy metal without the cliched chords, it had a great intro riff, was well constructed, original and well performed. I turned to my partner and said, "They've nailed it and it will win!"

After the different countries' "establishment" juries had their says my choice was not looking good, the juries choosing two ballads. The French entry was well performed in the Edith Piaf style but hardly had the wow factor so I still hoped the public would see sense.

Thank goodness they did! The only thing I can agree with the "juries" about was zero points for the UK.

Yours,

R.A.S.

Here is another e-mail sent to Pincher to which he actually replied:

Dear Mr Pincher,

Over the next few years we are going to, hopefully, drift away from the internal combustion engine as a means of driving our vehicles to the much more eco-friendly electric motor, but what really concerns me is that these vehicles will have very little associated sound with them. I remember a few years ago reading that the EU were going to bring in legislation on these vehicles requiring them to only "sound" if they were reversing. At the time I thought this was completely bonkers and I still do. I envisage absolute carnage on the roads if we adopt the same policy as the EU proposed. Besides decimating the wildlife when they try crossing roads at night, I suspect many blind people will also succumb to this silent killer. Please say government are not going to be as stupid as the EU.

Yours,

R.A.S.

Pincher replied with the following statements:

(a) that in 2019 the Government secured new regulations to address these concerns. He then goes on to talk about acoustic sound systems.

(b) he says that from July 2021 the new regulations will cover both electric and hybrid vehicles.

(c) he then specifies these new regulations. Apparently these acoustic sound systems only appear to be necessary for reversing and for speeds BELOW 12mph...WHAT!!! and what's more they can be disabled at will!!!

If only we lived in a world where people limited their vehicle speed to below 12mph, wouldn't that be wonderful!!! Am I living on the same planet as these total buffoons that are drawing up these rules???

The BBC and possibly the Guardian received this e-mail in the summer of 2021. There was no response from either organisations:

On Thursday 17th June I looked at the BBC weather predictions for the next few days in my area and was happy that there was little probability of rain until the following Sunday morning. No surprise then that Friday there was a torrential deluge that continued throughout the whole day!!! This is a continuing problem with BBC weather forecasts... they are, basically, rubbish! They cannot even predict the following day's heavy rain! I'm not sure where the BBC is getting its weather information from but in recent years it has got progressively worse. I remember a few years ago that the weathermen had invested a huge amount of money in a super computer that was going to predict the weather 14 days ahead of time ...so what happened there then!

To say that I am not enamoured with the BBC and their weather predictions would be an understatement as this piece from 2008 proves:

The BBC Weather (Disinformation) Show

Well could you ever have believed that a programme like the BBC Weather Show could be used as a vehicle for disinformation? Smiley, smiley Carol Kirkwood fronts a programme full of her smiley, smiley weather presenters oozing reassurances over the effects of global warming. We are shown a simplistic map of the globe with two white blobs at the top and bottom to represent the north and south poles and are told by the smiling presenter about what the effect of the melting of these two areas might have on sea levels. Reassuringly the presenter had spent two and a half years under Antarctic ice, so we are all supposed to be happy he knows what he is talking about! He then goes on to tell us about the effects of the melting Arctic icecap, in which he compares this monumental event with the mundane occurrence of a cube of ice melting in a glass of water. He tells us that because this icecap does not cover any land mass it will hardly affect world sea levels. What he failed to discuss is the bloody great land mass of Greenland (conveniently NOT coloured white) next to the Arctic icecap with its huge area of rapidly melting mountains of ice!!!

He continues by discussing the effects that a melting Antarctic might have on sea-levels; telling us about how this ice sheet only covers a "few islands" as though the land mass under the Antarctic was of little significant size, and finally concludes the whole business by implying that global warming effects are two or three hundred years down the line anyway …so no worries then!

The programme continues with the ever smiling Carol Kirkwood having a jolly good time around the aviation industry (what a girl she is! How reassuring it is to know that this knowledgeable professional has no hang ups at all about air travel and its contribution to global warming).

I could hardly suppress my seething anger by the time two other smiley, smiley weathermen tell us that the Institute of Hydrology and whoever have (fortunately) come to the conclusion that last year's flooding was not caused by global warming at all, but was just a freak event; presumably similar in its freakishness to the one that occurred at Boscastle only a couple of years earlier!!!

And those Carol Kirkwood outtakes at the end of the programme defy description; I was really rolling out of my chair by then.

Once upon a time the BBC was an impartial observer and reporter of world events; clearly, like a stable climate, those days are long gone!!!

Yours sincerely

R.A.S.

Here is another weather-related e-mail to the BBC sent during the summer of 2021:

On the 19th June 2021 I e-mailed to the Guardian and the BBC complaining about the continual inaccuracies in the BBC's Weather forecasting. Well, since that e-mail, the saga continues with many more poor "guesses" by the BBC forecasters. Yesterday, for instance, I checked the local forecast for the next few days and there was no indication whatsoever of any rain on the horizon; however, today (14/08/21) we suffered an absolute deluge for about three hours in the afternoon.

Now what really concerns me is the amount of broadcasting time on all of the BBC channels that is devoted to these useless bits of guesswork. Can't we just replace the weather "person" with the good old fashioned interlude showing pleasant country scenes or even the potter's wheel!

No response from the "Beeb" again.

This correspondence was sent to both the local newspaper and Pincher:

It was a pleasant day in late August when Pam and I decided to go for a walk along the canal. It was initially going to be a walk of about 4 miles culminating in a visit to Sainsbury in Ventura Park for a midday meal. However, when we got to the turn-off to Ventura Park we decided to carry on to Hopwas and feed at the Red Lion pub. Shortly after the turn-off we passed several fields of sweetcorn on the south side of the canal which was very pleasing to my eye, but further along on the towpath side and to the north of the canal there was the noise of heavy machinery helping to construct yet another housing estate around the once attractive rural village of Tamworth. We continued our walk along the canal to Hopwas (an enclave that I've no doubt will soon be absorbed into an ever-expanding Tamworth) and ate at the pub.

We decided to retrace our steps back along the canal after we had finished our meal and on the walk back we encountered an old lady exercising her old tired-looking dog just by the new housing development. She was brandishing a walking stick in the air at the earthmover just the other side of the hedgerow that was part of the work going on there and she was uttering some very unladylike expletives. This lady had probably lived in the area most of her life and had watched as the village of Tamworth had slowly but surely encroached into her domain. Her surroundings were now going to be full of little brick boxes full of people she did not know who were, in all probability, holding none of her views or beliefs. Having spent many years campaigning to try and prevent the Anker Valley housing estate being built, my sympathies were totally with this old woman and her outrage.

I was born in Birmingham and lived within 4 miles of the city centre and during my early life was within half a mile of a farmer's fields. Over my lifetime I have seen Birmingham stretch many miles beyond those fields and am now watching the same repeat story operating in Tamworth. This concrete cancer is stretching across the Midlands, across the country, across the Earth...this is NOT progress, this is a prelude to the destruction of this planet!

R.A.S.

This e-mail did not get printed in the Herald as far as I am aware but did invoke a response from Pincher ...he was after all Housing Minister at that time!

In his reply letter he gives the usual spiel about local residents having the right to raise objections, propose amendments and confirm approval...I don't think that old dear had much of an input here.

He tells us that the development was designed by Lichfield District Council and in a referendum gained an 86% approval vote.

Well once again we have a situation here, like the Browns Lane development, where we have the adjoining Conservative Borough Council in Lichfield (and, of course, we also have a fellow Conservative MP in Lichfield) deciding to dump their required housing developments as far away from the centre of Lichfield as they can, and where they can utilize Tamworth services in the development of these sites!

Pincher also describes, sympathetically, the concerns of Hopwas locals to the development and then says the neighbourhood plan factors in local farmland that could potentially be used for future development!!

He then takes a swipe at the Labour Party and says there will be no repeat of the 60s brutalism you saw in Birmingham.

The man really is becoming a complete ******.

Here is a very short e-mail sent to Pincher that received a one and a half page reply:

Dear Sir/ Madam,

I notice that the Home Secretary is, via the police, going to ankle tag some environmental protesters ...a group of people that are showing more concern about the future of the planet than any politician ...my question is...are they also going to be ankle tagging police sex offenders?

Yours,

R.A.S.

Pincher replied with standard government speak on the subject of environmental protesters with two short paragraphs, but spent over one page of A4 talking about the sexual side of my question! In view of his own subsequent behaviour there seems to be a great deal of irony in this response!

Next we return to football and an e-mail I sent to our local newspaper and Tamworth FC:

Well, it was Saturday afternoon and I was eliminated from the Ascot placepot on the second race, so when my partner, Pam, suggested we go to the Lamb to watch Tamworth play Notts County in an FA cup qualifying round, I said "Why not".

It had been seven or eight years since we last watched Tamworth play, so the trip would be interesting and informative.

We bought concession tickets from the shop and the price of £9 each was about the same that we paid several years before, so that was a plus, however what followed was not so good.

On the terraces at the far end we had a good view of the pitch and I soon noticed it was now artificial and not the grass covered ground of previous visits. Unfortunately we stood close to an elderly and extremely vocal "supporter" who insisted on giving everyone his interpretation of the events taking place on the pitch. Moving away would not be easy until half-time as the place was packed (a bigger crowd than I could recall on any previous visit).

Now this is where it gets even more disappointing, at half-time there was NO interval music, there was NO half-time score announcements from other games and NO ticket number lucky draw announcement. (My ticket number was 01238 so I'm sure the club could afford a decent prize draw!)

From our new vantage point we watched the remainder of the game amidst hordes of yelling children who seemed to have very little interest in what was taking place on the football pitch, but, at least, that was a bit better than the loud-mouthed "gentleman" we had to endure during the first half. As for the events on the pitch, the most noticeable observation was that the Notts County goalkeeper, Patterson, insisted on spending most of the game as near to the halfway line as possible...he was a complete clown...but a greater clown was the Tamworth coach/manager who failed to exploit this idiot's antics!!!

We will NOT be going to the Lamb again in the foreseeable future.

R.A.S.

There was, understandably, no reply from Tamworth FC and the story was not printed in the Herald.

This message was probably not sent to anyone and was clearly written when I was in a rather depressed mood. It is an over emotive piece of work:

Climate Change

What we need is WAR WAR not JAW JAW. We need to make war on all those that promote the use of fossil fuels; that includes all petrol-heads, the likes of Lewis Hamilton and all his fellow Formula One drivers and television programmes like Top Gear; it also includes the likes of Michael O'Leary, Willie Walsh and other airline barons that advocate limitless air travel. These people always hide behind their staff and associates by pleading that there are so many people's jobs that are dependent on their continued existence...bollocks...these creeps are only interested in their own fat-cat lifestyles. The people that work in these fossil-fuel consuming professions should look into their children and grandchildren's eyes and explain to them what their occupations are doing to the planet that these children are going to grow up in!

Every time you put your foot down on the accelerator pedal you are putting your foot down onto your child or grandchild's head!

Every time you board a plane you should realize that you are helping to kill hundreds of thousands in future climate-induced famines!

These words are from someone who spent 12 years in the RAF and used a motorcycle for transport for most of his early life...but I was truly ignorant of what I was doing to the planet; however, by the turn of the century I saw "the light" by personal experience and what science was telling me.

Those that persist in their use of fossil-fuel consuming non-essential occupations or lifestyles now have absolutely NO excuse for their behaviour ...YOU know precisely what YOU are doing!!

Yours,

R.A.S.

This was sent to the BBC and once again received no reply:

Universe!

More fanciful, over-dramatic claptrap from Cox...why do I watch it?...Well, there is the odd snippet of useful information that is presented that I can't be bothered to look up in any children's basic astronomy book.

How does he continue to get away with these "science" series? For a large percentage of His programmes we are transported into His particular mental meanderings that, for the most part, have only a flimsy connection to reality, and are expounded in contrived grandeur on some lofty peak in yet another far-away location! I assume that his friends at the BBC decide which is the next exotic mountainous location we can let Cox and his entourage loose on, in order to say his next (very few) "earth-shattering" words! I'm all in favour of imagination...I have made many useful and functional items using my imagination and what is possible with the components available at the time, but Cox is on a different planet as far as imagination goes!

Please, please, mercy I'm 76... no more Cox, he's doing my head in!... let's have proper science programmes please!

R.A.S.

Around this time that bit of annual nonsense concerned with global warming had started in Glasgow (COP 26) and an announcement by the British and American governments engendered this response and was sent to the usual people:

Flights to America

Are YOU all F***ING insane in reinstating flights to America.

I am 76 (spent 12 years in the RAF) and lost faith in humanity years ago but did have a glimmer of hope with the advent of COP 26...how misguided I was!

While this farce in Glasgow is still going on we and the Americans decide to get back on to the path of planetary destruction...unbelievable!

Those airway "fat cats" win again; and I am just told on the BBC news that, according to some, there are over 500 delegates at Glasgow with links to the petro-chemical industry...no surprise there then!

People that can afford to fly to America can spend their money on electronics to skype their loved-ones instead; particularly in today's pandemic climate!

Yours,

R.A.S.

This e-mail was quickly followed by a follow-up e-mail:

Flights to America (CORRECTION)

In a previous correspondence to yourselves I made an error for which I apologise. I suggested that an item on the BBC news had indicated that an outside organization had alleged that there were over 500 delegates at COP26 with links to the petro-chemical industry...that was untrue; it was my purple-faced anger at re-establishing flights to America that overcame me and led to this distortion. What the BBC report actually said was that an outside organization had alleged that there were over 500 delegates at COP26 with links to the fossil fuel industry. I always endeavour to be accurate in what I say even if you and the rest of humanity ignores my prophecies of impending doom! (see "Memories of a grey-haired old Brummie" for further information!)

R.A.S.

More vitriol from me, this time about Remembrance Day:

I spent 12 years in the RAF and I have a great deal of sympathy for all those injured in past conflicts, but what is happening to the Remembrance Day celebrations at the Cenotaph? There were tens of thousands of people in the march past ...how long will it be before the Walthamstow Dog Track Old Boys Association is represented there! It is getting really absurd! As for the wreath laying ceremony, I notice it is still following the usual "pecking" order, with the lesser beings laying their wreaths after the rich and famous have done their bit; but what I really find upsetting about the whole thing is the fact that all these thousands have assembled at the Cenotaph after travelling some distance and, in the process, have expelled huge quantities of CO_2 into the atmosphere!

I understand that we need to pay homage to those that have fallen in previous wars and conflicts but what is much more important is our children's future...and to anyone who bangs on about "learning the lessons of the past" with such parades, I say that will NEVER happen, but what will DEFINITELY happen is more human misery with the advent of more global warming due to totally unnecessary CO_2 emissions!

Ron S.

I am not proud of this e-mail but it was sent to Pincher anyway:

Dear Mr Pincher,

I have written to you on many occasions and I am sure you may have got the impression that I am a serial moaner; however, finding fault is an extension of what the Royal Air Force trained me to do, and that was to find the faults in inoperable pieces of radar equipment, and I have, unfortunately, tended to extend my fault finding to most aspects of human behaviour, as you well know!

My particular grouse at the moment concerns my local medical practice, namely The Hollies.

Let me say from the start that nobody, but nobody, is more of a supporter of the NHS than I...my partner had one hip replacement and the other re-surfaced and it made an enormous difference to the quality of her life; I was helped by the NHS to recover from two separate episodes of pulmonary embolisms and my step-grandson who had to have a cardiac operation when he was only two or three weeks old is now a bouncing 4 year old...so no-one can be more grateful to the NHS than I!

However, my postponed annual check-up (because of my use of anti-coagulants) that was due to take place at 10:40 today was not completed because I walked out at 11:10, having felt that this was too long a delay considering the lack of patients in the waiting area.

May I explain further: pre-pandemic my annual appointments were, despite crowded waiting areas, always conducted on time or often even before time.

What concerns me now is that my local medical practice, which I entered for the first time in over 18 months and is like entering the "Marie Celeste", is, in some way "cashing in" on the pandemic to ease their work load and reduce their efficiency; moreover the number of GPs seems to have grown considerably since I was last there but there was hardly anyone waiting to be seen...why?

Now, of course, they have a million excuses with the onset of coronavirus...staff off ill, overworked doctors etc. etc., but the chasm between what was and what is makes this old fault-finder wonder!

Yours,

Ron S.

I know Pincher replied to this one but, unfortunately, I have been unable to find his reply letter; however, from what I can remember of his response he was not best pleased! He was particularly unhappy with the suggestion that the practice was in some way cashing in on the pandemic to ease their workload…he was, probably, correct in sending me this reprimand!

Now this e-mail sent to nearly everyone, including Pincher, gave us further evidence of the Conservative Party's complete incompetence. It had shown itself incompetent, of course, with Pincher himself. Here was a shy, retiring (and possibly sensitive) soul who the Party machine had elevated from the Backbenches to High Office and with it allowed him great powers that, eventually, proved far too much for the man! Anyway, here is the e-mail:

Dear Sir/Madam (and Pincher),

Over the past year or so we have all been an audience to habitual Conservative incompetence, and this incompetence was highlighted even more by their selection of the candidate to represent their party at the North Shropshire by-election.

Instead of selecting a local "safe" Conservative candidate they opted for importing someone from Birmingham of all places and with some ethnic origins to boot! Talk about sending someone into the lion's den!

North Shropshire is a rural constituency with traditional views and beliefs so how on earth was this particular candidate ever going to succeed there?

I'm a Brummie, born and bred, and I've no doubt this promising candidate would have gone down a storm in Erdington, Kingstanding, Small Heath, Edgbaston etc. etc...but rural Shropshire...no way!...yet even more Tory incompetence on display here then!

R.A.S.

Naturally I received no response from anyone on this one!

The next short e-mail was sent to the BBC, the Guardian and Pincher:

Dear Sir/ Madam (and Pincher),

As the Prime Minister continues to flounder on questions about his personal behaviour, what really upset me at today's PMQs was his attempt to suggest that all those that had booster jabs were in some way endorsing his leadership ...what depths will he descend to next to save his premiership???

Yours,

R.A.S.

Here's another e-mail sent to all on Boris's behaviour:

Outrageous, outrageous, outrageous!!!

How can I use the system for more obfuscation and more delay? What mechanism can I use?...Ah! I know!

Why not get the police involved as this will automatically trigger a delay in the release of the Sue Gray report!

This will allow me to cling on to my office for a few more weeks and hopefully a war in Ukraine will again help me (like many other floundering Prime Ministers or Presidents have done before) out of the huge hole I find myself in!

Does this Prime Minister really believe that he can continue to hoodwink the general public indefinitely??

God help us if he can!!!

Yours,

R.A.S.

These two e-mails seemed to trigger a two and a half page response from Pincher, a reply that the law prevents me from duplicating here; however, I will try to give you the gist of what he said.

The first paragraph says that he appreciates my thoughts on current events and that he has read my e-mails thoroughly.

The second paragraph explains the government's great battle with Covid 19 and all the extraordinary processes that they have had to go through to keep us all safe.

The third paragraph is a condemnation of those that had broken the rules during the pandemic and an expression of his own personal ignorance of any goings on in connection with "partygate"...nothing to do with me, guv!

The fourth paragraph expresses his confidence in the integrity of Sue Gray and that her initial report has now been delivered to the PM who has made it universally available online; however, her full report would not be available until the police have concluded their investigations. He talks about lessons to be learned already...blah blah blah.

The fifth paragraph describes the geography of No.10 and how this could have been important in the goings on there, and that there is a small flat at the top of the building that he personally has never entered...shame!

The sixth paragraph describes how we have all suffered during the pandemic. How both he and the PM have both had a dose and that how the PM's mother had died and yet the PM still chaired a Cabinet meeting the following day...what a guy! He explains that the PM also had worries about his newborn who also contracted Covid.

Paragraph no.7 explained how he had personally gone out and investigated the feelings of Tamworth locals, and how there were world events that were making life difficult for us all. Of course, despite all the many Conservative indiscretions over the year, Pincher has to have another dig at the Labour Party because of a Labour MP associated with Chinese money...this is a standard Pincher ploy!

The last paragraph tells us that the PM "gets it" and that we must all get on and GO GO GO!...yeah, yeah, yeah!

The following e-mail was sent to Pincher in response to the lengthy letter he had sent to me. There is clearly a grave mistake on my part in that I called him Deputy Leader of the House rather than his real title of Deputy Chief Whip, but maybe he was flattered by this error. Anyway this what was sent:

Dear Mr Pincher,

I am not on the web in any of its many forms and am really quite a private person and when I have something to say of importance to me I e-mail to you, the Guardian or the BBC and, to your credit, you are the only one that has the decency to respond to some of my concerns. Your latest reply to my questions about "partygate" was quite lengthy so I will share with you, at length, some of my other concerns and as the new deputy Leader of the House I hope you will take some of them "on board":

(1) An issue has arisen recently about what children in primary schools should be taught. I would like to say that I am totally and completely opposed to introducing politics in any form to children of this age! Their curriculum should really be concerned with the three "Rs", science and nature, and nothing more. Despite what others think, I do not believe that children of this age have their own opinions about stuff, and what they have to say always reflects opinions held by their teachers, parents, the media or other family members.

I did not become "politically aware" until Thatcher forced her thoughts into my way of life in the early eighties...I was in my late thirties at that time!

(2) The Ukraine issue...I wrote to you in 2014 with my concerns about the Crimea issue and you replied then to my thoughts.

Since then my opinions about what is happening in that part of the world have not changed:

(a) This issue is being fermented as a diversion by Western leaders who have their own considerable internal problems to deal with.

(b) As raised with you in 2014, I highlighted the hypocrisy of the USA in their involvement in this region when they had a recent history themselves of invading sovereign states, namely Grenada and Panama!

(c) I have always had my doubts about NATO. It was set up (with the USA being the driving force) as mostly a joint effort with other European countries to deter any possible Russian aggression; however, I suspect that Europe is, in reality, the first line of defence in protecting the Americans from any conflict with Russia...we, in Europe, are merely cannon fodder for the USA!

(3) Overriding all of these issues is the most important issue of all... that of tackling Global Warming. Anyone who has any concern at all for future generations must realize that this is the number one priority for every country in the world. Unfortunately, I am a total pessimist on this topic as tackling this problem relies on politicians and they are the representatives of their peoples...and the people are WRONG...they continue to want their cars and their flights abroad and their selfish lifestyles which have profound and catastrophic effects on the planet... we simply cannot square this circle!!!

Yours,

R.A.S.

This following e-mail was sent to the usual crew but also Lisa Nandy of the Labour Party:

Dear Sir/Madam (and Lisa),

Once again we have a member of the Labour party talking through his arse.

David Lammy is in favour of an open door to Ukrainian refugees... he is clearly trying to politically "cash-in" on public sympathy for the Ukrainian situation.

This gentleman simply cannot see the end of his nose; does he not realize that the future holds out the prospect of more and more mass migrations for various reasons...are we to treat these future refugees to his open door policy?

If we are to follow his (opportune) rantings there will be increased pressure on our housing stock and public services, to the detriment of future generations in this country!!

Yours,

R.A.S.

I had no response from anyone. Hardly surprising that Lisa Nandy did not reply as Lammy has inherited her old job!

This again was another general e-mail:

> I've never tried to disguise my intense dislike and distrust of America, the American people and the American way of life.
>
> I'm old enough to remember Grenada, Panama and even the Cuban missile crisis, where an American president was prepared to risk a world-wide nuclear holocaust to protect HIS patch and HIS sphere of influence. (With the advent of ICBMs a few years later, what a total waste of time and space that Cuban nonsense turned out to be!)
>
> Now we have yet another loony POLITICIAN who wants to defend HIS patch and HIS sphere of influence with an invasion of a neighbouring country... what the hell is he expecting to achieve?
>
> Every Ukrainian life he takes will eventually come back to haunt him and his country. There will be tens of thousands dead (maybe even more) and every one of the dead will have relatives that survive and many of those will be Russian-speaking and will have no difficulty at all in finding their way into St Petersburg or Moscow with their truck loads of explosives to inflict on the Russian people what they have suffered.
>
> Now, of course, this is where it will become very messy because the trapped rat Putin or his successor will now blame the West for these incursions and then the you-know-what will really hit the fan!

A leopard doesn't change its spots and the human race will NEVER change ...whether it be allowing loony POLITICIANS to lead them or, just as important, not conquering Global Warming.

Yours,

R.A.S.

Another general e-mail, football orientated this time:

Dear Sir/ Madam,

It is absolutely OUTRAGEOUS that the Football Association decided to go ahead with staging the semi-final between two teams from the Northwest at Wembley!

Clearly the people that run this organization have NO respect for anything apart from THEIR own self-interest.

They do not care about their children or grandchildren that are going to have to pick up the pieces from the effects of Global Warming!

The decision makers in the FA could have re-arranged this fixture to a neutral ground in the Northwest and saved many more hundreds of tons of CO_2 being dumped into the atmosphere...are they all completely INSANE!

Yours,

R.A.S.

Back to politics again with this e-mail sent to everyone:

Dear Sir/Madam,

WHITEWASH! WHITEWASH! NO! GRAYWASH!!!

The recently released Gray Report told us absolutely nothing we did not already know; however, what is interesting is what is NOT in the report, namely a gathering that took place in the PM's own apartment.

It was reported that Gray did not investigate this gathering because a recently established Police enquiry had just overtaken her on this issue, how very convenient!!!

Yes, clearly Boris is definitely her boss!

As far as I am aware this particular episode was NOT addressed by the police and if it was addressed NO fine resulted for the PM.

Yours,

R.A.S.

No response from anyone.

This is an e-mail, whose eventual reply from Pincher gave me cause to think something might not be quite right with the man. It concerned yet another American school massacre, this time in Uvalde, Texas:

More American Insanity.

Dear Sir/Madam (and Pincher),

I was born just before the first Atomic bombs were dropped on civilians in Japan by the Americans and since that time there have been numerous events and incidents in my life that have led me to a belief that the USA is a country that is not to be trusted (or to be looked up to) under any circumstances.

In a world that has an increasing number of "loonies on the loose" this country seems to have a disproportionately higher number compared with other countries in the world.

This factor combined with a country awash with firearms is bound to lead to the obscenity that occurred in Uvalde, Texas.

Yours,

R.A.S.

This e-mail received a reply from Pincher dated 21/06/2022 and in it he uses the first two paragraphs of the reply to extol the virtues of our Anglo-American relationship, which, of course, went completely against the grain with me. However, it was the third paragraph that troubled me. Despite me e-mailing him about the deaths of schoolchildren by gunfire, and how abhorrent I found it, he feels it appropriate to suggest that I might, possibly, be interested in joining a local clay shooting range to learn more about gun use…surely he knows by now that I am an elderly ex-serviceman and would know all I need to know about firearms! Clearly I found this last paragraph both distasteful and strange! Is he losing it, I wondered.

I was so keen to make sure that this next e-mail was published in our local newspaper that I made a hard copy and attempted to take the letter to the offices of our newspaper in Ventura Park...**and this is where the whole world starts to collapse**...here is the relevant document:

Dear Sir/Madam,

Many years ago my partner and I were among the founders of "Friends of Warwickshire Moor" and we endeavoured to give local people a pleasant retreat to visit, when life got tough. We initially maintained the area along Moor Lane on a fortnightly basis, but in recent years that has been reduced to a monthly regime due to us all getting older and less mobile.

A few years ago I quit my monthly duties due to an increase in the number of attacks on the site by vandals, including the burning down of part of the boardwalk by the river...it just angered me so much!

However, three or four years ago I re-engaged with the group and continued helping despite the outbreaks of "summer vandalism", which continued to go unchecked and UNPUNISHED.

Now, once again, we are faced with another spate of seasonal lunacy.

Recently we have had signage sprayed over with red paint and now once AGAIN the dipping platform has been destroyed by fire.

Clearly these "mindless morons" have absolutely no respect for their community or the law. This is hardly surprising since those holding the highest positions in our society seem to have a similar lack of respect for their people and the LAW!

Yours,

R.A.S.

It was eventually printed in the Herald but stuff happened before it was printed.

You see when I arrived in the pouring rain at what used to be the office of our local newspaper it was no longer there and prompted this angry and factually inaccurate e-mail to Pincher:

Dear Mr Pincher,

You cannot believe how angry I am at the moment, having just been caught in a rainstorm whilst trying to deliver a letter, concerning our vandalised boardwalk, to the offices of the Tamworth Herald in Ventura Park...only to discover that there are no longer any offices representing this newspaper in Tamworth, and everything has to go through the Birmingham Mail, some 21 miles away.

I am a Brummie born and bred so I have no hang ups about Birmingham, but when I arrived in Tamworth some 35 years ago there were TWO independent local newspapers and now under your watch there are NONE!

I am upset about the vandalism on our Nature Reserve but am just as upset about our local news being vetted, edited and CONTROLLED by people 21 miles away in Birmingham.

This state of affairs has happened under your watch and even though I am now a rickety old 77 year old, I will make it my aim to stop you being elected at the next General Election!

I am pretty good with placards and walking up and down High Streets as the delay to the building of the Anker Valley estate will testify... unless you find some way to knobble me, your days as an MP for this constituency are numbered!

Yours,

R.A.S.

P.S. A few weeks ago I went through the Birmingham Mail to try and get an innocuous and complimentary letter concerning my partner's 80th birthday at a local hotel published in the Tamworth Herald...to my knowledge it never saw the light of day!

I also decided to send a copy of this e-mail to Dan Newbould, editor of the Tamworth Herald, which initiated an immediate response from him in which he denied being based in Birmingham and said that he was definitely based in Tamworth.

All this happened on Monday 27th June 2022.

Two days later on the evening of the 29th June Pincher decides to go
out and get pissed and revert to type in the Carlton Club.

On the morning of that very day, my anger with the world and Pincher
continued with the following letter sent first class to the Tamworth
Borough Councillor, Marie Bailey:

Dear Marie,

I have looked on the GOV.UK website concerning the Permission to
distribute leaflets (England and Wales) and it suggests that you should
"check with your council to see if you need permission to distribute
free printed material in England and Wales".

However, later it suggests "you do NOT need permission if the printed
material is being distributed;

in letterboxes

inside a building, bus or taxi

on behalf of a charity

for POLITICAL or religious purposes or other beliefs".

So, to be clear if I distributed leaflets in Ankerside (inside a building)
against the re-election of our local Member of Parliament (political
purposes) in the run-up to the next General Election would I be free

to do so, or would I be committing an offence in some way.(unlike the Prime Minister I am anxious not to break the LAW in any way).

Yours,

R.A.S.

I have NEVER received a reply to this e-mail.

Now this is pure speculation, but could the e-mail sent to Pincher two days earlier, caused a reaction in him on that Wednesday that eventually led to turmoil in the Conservative Party and the downfall of Boris!

You see I believe Pincher, underneath, to be a sensitive soul (far too sensitive to hold High Office) and that the old local man that he had been having dialogue with ever since being elected to represent Tamworth was now turning against him (with intent), may have been too much for him and caused his actions on the evening of the 29th June.

Clearly this is all speculation but does, I believe, have a degree of credibility.

Anyway despite what was happening in the "Westminster Bubble" I continued my e-mailing. This one was to the Tamworth Herald, a toned-down version of which was printed in the paper:

Dear Daniel,

I would like to make it perfectly clear to you that I do not give a sh*t about Mr Pincher's sexual orientation or about him getting pissed in some London club...however, if he has made improper and unwanted advances to others that is a totally different matter altogether.

Throughout his entire time as our MP I have e-mailed him on numerous occasions about issues that concern me, and to his great credit he has often replied to me (and, of course, quite often ducked the more contentious e-mails). This contrasts to e-mails sent to both the BBC and the Guardian on similar issues, which have NEVER been either replied to or printed! A recent reply from Mr Pincher to one of my e-mails did give me some concern about his general well-being though!

I will do what I can to prevent him from another term as our MP because I feel he has not served Tamworth well or addressed many of my concerns positively during the past twelve years.

Yours,

R.A.S.

With the resignation of Boris on the 7th July I sent this somewhat triumphalist e-mail to the editor of the Herald knowing full well it would never be printed:

Dear Daniel,

Talk about the "Butterfly Effect"!

As you know I sent Mr Pincher an e-mail on Monday 27th June suggesting that I would do all I could to prevent him gaining another term as our MP at the next General Election and that his "days were numbered"!

Lo and behold on the following Wednesday evening he decides to go out and get pissed at some London club and, once again, revert to type. (To suggest that this episode was related in some way to my e-mail would be absurdly pretentious and highly improbable but it would make the basis for a good book!)

This lapse by Pincher has now led to the collapse of our ruling party and the demise of Boris!

Unbelievable!!!

R.A.S.

In mid-July 2022 I continued e-mailing with this effort to our local newspaper:

Dear Daniel,

I objected to the Anker Valley development as early as 2001 and increased my activity on this topic when the idea was resurrected (along with a new area around Browns Lane) in 2007/2008.

Since that time, under Pincher and the Conservatives, we have had these areas concreted over, along with our golf course and a huge area around Dunstall Lane. (Incidentally, Pincher claims to be a member of the Hodge Lane Nature Reserve, yet allowed the concreting over of the adjacent golf course and the subsequent loss of wildlife habitat without the slightest objection!)

Now there is a new development proposed called Grangewood Park... and the "madness continues"!

If you can be bothered to look up the Herald archives you will see many pieces I have written on this subject and I draw your attention to a piece I wrote in around 2007/2008 which is as relevant now as it was then!

So far we have been extremely lucky in Tamworth not to get the sort of flooding experienced in other parts of Europe, but it is only a matter of time before we get the "big one" aided, of course, by all the run-off from all of these housing developments!!!

Yours,

R.A.S.

There was a follow-up e-mail sent to Daniel (Herald) a few days later on the same subject:

Dear Dan,

In case you could not be bothered to look up old Herald archives, here is a copy of what I wrote for the Herald in 2007/2008 which I consider to be as relevant now as it was then:

"Yes it's me again banging on about flooding in Tamworth yet again. It seems as though I have spent an eternity writing to the Herald, local councillors, planning departments, our MP and the Environment Agency on this issue.

I am doing my very best to make people see the demonstrable link between concreting over green field sites and the increased chances of flooding in our area. The facts readers need to know are as follows:

(1) Only 31% of rainfall that falls in Europe actually finds its way into our water courses in normal circumstances, the rest is lost back into the atmosphere via evaporation and transpiration, or through helping plants grow or migration through the ground into the water table. Now when you concrete over a green field site there is NO transpiration, there is NO plant growth, there is NO soak away and unless it is a hot and windy day very little evaporation. So practically all the rainfall finds its way into the nearest watercourse.

(2) Tamworth is at the junction of two rivers, both of whom serve as drains for huge areas of concreted over land; namely (part of)

Birmingham in the case of the Tame, and Nuneaton, Atherstone, Polesworth and part of the M42 in the case of the Anker.

(3) This recent flooding event did NOT occur through some terrific downpour. According to my rain gauge approximately 65mm of rain fell in six days prior to this flooding event. This is hardly world shattering rainfall when you consider the serious rainfall events all over the country over the past five years so Heaven help us when we cop for one of these!

No, we have been lucky yet again; planners and Environment Agency please note!"

I think (2) above to be highly significant for Tamworth with future climate change uncertainties becoming oh so apparent!

R.A.S.

On the 20th July I totally unexpectedly received a delayed letter from Pincher dated 29/6/2022 the VERY day of his indiscretions and led to the following e-mail to Daniel (Herald):

Dear Daniel,

Yesterday I received a delayed letter from our Member of Parliament dated 29th June...an EXTREMELY significant date in the life of the Rt. Hon. Christopher Pincher MP (and, incidentally, for the whole of the country).

It expresses sympathy for me getting wet on my walk and then tells me that the reporter for our area, Dan Newbould, is a man "that lives and breathes" Tamworth and is definitely not based in Birmingham City Centre. Now, strangely, when you e-mailed me on the 27th June you used exactly the same expression: ie that you live and breathe the town, and you were definitely not based in Birmingham.

Anyway, he goes on to say "I disagree entirely that The Tamworth Herald is not independent, as you may know, it is owned by Reach PLC who also own titles like the Mirror, Sunday Mirror, Daily Star and others"...and continues to say that none of these newspapers are very sympathetic to the Conservatives or the Government.

WHAT!! Clearly the definition of "independent" is multifaceted but when used in connection with a newspaper most people would say that independent meant "not associated with or owned by a larger business" so I just don't get Pincher's reasoning and as for the political orientation of the papers he has listed...what has that got to do with the price of fish!

Yours,

R.A.S.

Clearly his lack of understanding of the word "independent" shows his muddled thinking on that eventful day and his reference to unsympathetic papers clearly betray a feeling in him of political insecurity and persecution.

Now these quotes I have given from his letter to me might well get me into hot water, but I feel they are necessary for an understanding of Pincher's possible internal turmoil on that day!

About this time I wrote a couple of e-mails to the Herald in which I suggested that future sea-level rises might cause an increase in the possibilities of flooding in Tamworth, but after due consideration felt that this was probably not a valid hypothesis.

After the success of the Lionesses in the European Championship I sent this e-mail to the rest of the world without response:

Dear Dan (and others),

Many congratulations to the Lionesses, they were terrific, but, unlike my partner, I am "a glass is half empty" sort of a guy and do, now, fear for the future of women's football.

At the moment, going to watch a ladies' football match is totally testosterone-free; you can take your daughter or your family without being harassed, listen to obscene chanting or watch irresponsible pitch invasions...but will it stay like that for the girls?

My fear is that as our overpaid male game continues to disappoint, particularly on an international level, the female game will start to be invaded by more and more of these testosterone-fuelled "fans" that now prevent many normal families from going to watch our national game!

E-mails were sent to three of our local councillors which went as follows:

(1) The content of this section related to my letter to a fellow councillor, Marie Bailey, and emphasised that I had still not received any reply from her.

(2) This section related to my delayed letter from Pincher.

(3) I have noticed in recent weeks there has been no mention whatsoever of our disgraced Member of Parliament in the Tamworth Herald ...are we trying to hide him away somewhere and then re-launch a new better-than-ever Christopher Pincher at the next General Election...God help us if that is the case!

(4) the report of the disgraceful behaviour of Tamworth FC supporters in attacking the Ilkeston FC coach (in which there were young children) was confined to a small section on page 3 in the Tamworth Herald, whereas the description of the game itself took up most of the back page. We all like to present Tamworth in a good light but playing down serious stuff like this is not good journalism!

R.A.S.

There was NO reply from any of the councillors.

After the death of the Queen I wrote this e-mail to the Herald:

Dear Daniel,

I am not particularly a royalist but no-one can deny the dedication and resilience of our late Queen; and of all the tributes given by the great and the good on television, the one anecdote that stood out for me was the one told by Clare Balding, which referred to the Queen as saying that she enjoyed her trips to the stables because it was one of the few places that she visited that did not smell of fresh paint!

Yours,

R.A.S.

After this innocuous Queen-related e-mail failed to get an entry into the letters section of the Herald and yet Pincher's did, I sent the following e-mail:

Dear Daniel,

I spent 12 years in the RAF serving Queen and country, and when I finished my engagement my character was described as "exemplary", so I was disappointed not to see the small piece I had written about our late Queen finding its way into the Herald.

Strangely, a gentleman who had served as our MP for a similar length of time as my service in the RAF left his office disgraced, and under a cloud of alleged bullying and sexual harassment...and yet he gets a nice little piece printed in the Herald in relation to our late Queen!

Once again the editorial integrity of yourself is brought into question, so much so that I will not be spending my hard earned £1.70 on the Herald ever again!

Yours for the last time,

R.A.S.

I had a very quick response from Mr. Newbould in which he says that he had been on holiday and was sorry my e-mail had been missed and that my e-mails would always be welcome. He then says that my e-mail would be printed in the next edition...and it was!

He followed up with an e-mail the following week by asking whether I had seen that my letter had been printed and that I should keep sending my e-mails in!

Here's one sent to the Herald that was not printed:

I am a scientist by nature and anything celestial is of interest to me; but the absurdity of NASA playing silly space games in trying to deflect the motion of a small asteroid under the pretext that the knowledge that they will gain from such an exercise could help us in any future threat of human annihilation by a rogue asteroid, is quite simply a totally misguided waste of time and money!

You wonder if a recent series of fanciful escapist films about asteroid impacts on the planet have affected the common sense and judgement of those running NASA!

If I were a bookmaker I would suggest that the odds of the human race being destroyed in the next 1,000 years by such an event are probably >10,000-1 against.

However, if you asked me about the future demise of the human race from a pandemic over the next millennium I would say probably <1,000-1 against; and if you are asking me about our future extinction through a nuclear holocaust over the same time period I would suggest a figure of <100-1 against (but with the likes of Putin or (heaven forbid) a resurrected Trump around, make that <10-1 against)...and, finally, if asked about the human race dying out within the next 1,000 years through the effects of global warming I would suggest the odds were shorter than even money!!!

This one went to both the BBC and the Guardian without reply of course:

When she was elected as Prime Minister I wrote that "little miss piggy has been elected to preside over the rotting corpse of her party...God help us all!"... unsurprisingly the BBC's "Have Your Say" did not let me have my say on this subject.

She replaced a proven LIAR and lasted just 44 days as PM after destroying our economy and our standing in the world. Now we are being told that the proven LIAR might be staging a bid to return to the Highest Office in the land with the support of many members of his party.

Can this country sink any lower? Where are our standards any more?

There are those in the Conservative Party that want to bring back the clown and are calling for the party to rally round and show complete and undying loyalty to him and his cause.

Does any of this remind you of the mentality of those that showed undying loyalty to many of the World's leading despots!

Yours,

R.A.S.

Amidst the chaos surrounding the resignation of little miss piggy I sent this e-mail to everyone:

Thank goodness, Boris is not going to run in yet another PM run off, contrary to what Rees-Mogg had declared to the World on Sunday!

Boris has probably withdrawn from the contest because he has not got the support and accolade that he had expected when he flew back from his Caribbean holiday, and probably also figures that any PM at this time faces an impossible task.

Now that the onerous task is probably going to fall on the shoulders of Rishi Sunak, I find it staggering how many high profile members of the Conservative Party crawl out of the woodwork to do 180 degree turns on their previous views to support him. It seems that to be a successful Conservative you need to have absolutely no principles of your own but just follow the herd until you find yourself in a rewarding high status position!

Yours,

Ron S.

About this time we had a piece in the Herald from our local council called Tamworth Today, in which they outlined their interpretation of what was going down in the town at this time. So I decided to send in my interpretation of Tamworth Today to the Herald. It was printed in the paper but was severely edited; here is the uncensored version:

We have read what our councillors believe is the state of Tamworth today, now I would like to introduce them to the reality from the standpoint of a 77 year old who has lived here for the past 35 years.

Where do I start?

Well probably the environment as this was an issue that I confronted the council with over twenty years ago. I continually opposed the building of the Anker Valley estate and that of another around Browns Lane (both on greenfield sites) because of the increased risk of flooding that this may cause to other areas of Tamworth in the future, and, of course, the loss of wildlife habitat. I often used letters in the Herald to further my arguments and anyone wishing to understand my reasoning can find them in the Herald archives.

Anyway since that time, under a Conservative controlled council we have had both sites built on along with our golf course and a large area around Dunstall Lane, all of which will undoubtedly contribute to a near certain future flooding event, and, unfortunately, has seen yet more wildlife displaced.

Clearly this race to build more houses is a certain way of generating more revenue for our councillors to play around with!

So what have they actually done with all this additional loot?

Well, on policing and law and order, the only thing that I have witnessed is the withdrawal of our police station from the centre of town where they used to be able to keep a close eye on weekend town centre revellers to some small outpost near Marlborough Way...well away from all of the weekend action! We have also seen the disappearance of Tamworth County Court despite an increased population in the area.

Now, on the subject of law and order, as a member of Friends of Warwickshire Moor, during the reign of Pincher and his Conservative run council I have witnessed habitual vandalism on our site (and have complained to Pincher many times) go totally unpunished. The latest of two burning downs of our dipping platform continues to go unpunished, and many promises of help from the council and Tamworth Lions remain in newspaper headlines ONLY!

Next we come to the NHS for the last twelve years.

There was a time back in the day when I could see my GP extremely easily and did not need to be computer-wise in order to arrange an appointment for a week or more ahead! In fact I have never even seen the GP that is now supposed to be looking after me!

Now I am 77 years old and my partner is 80 years old and yet we are forced to travel 60 miles across Birmingham to Solihull for routine check-ups that could quite easily be done at Robert Peel if there was an ounce of common sense involved...please explain, someone!

Next we come to local news and communication to the citizens of Tamworth.

Unfortunately, there is now only the Tamworth Herald to give us local information and the selection of news events in our area, and dare I say it, the slanting of news events seems to revolve around one person in particular. This is definitely not good or healthy for a balanced view of the town!

In my mind there is no question... we are on the road to nowhere!

Yours,

R.A.S.

Another e-mail sent without reply:

As you probably already know I despaired of humanity years ago and I am now resigned to our obvious fate as a species, by declining slowly into the abyss that awaits me.

However, there are those that still make my blood absolutely boil, many of whom are members of the Conservative Party and the House of Lords that still want to speed up our annihilation by clinging on to a carbon based energy policy, in order to placate their followers and ensure high returns on their own investments...live today, stuff tomorrow as I won't be around anyway seems to be their philosophy!

The problem is that most of them are old and decrepit and know that their own number is up shortly anyway so they have absolutely no concern about following their planet-destroying policies!

Not only do they have no thoughts for their children and grandchildren and certainly have no thoughts whatsoever for the collateral damage they are doing to other species that my contempt for them borders on hatred!

They want to carry on fiddling while Rome burns!!!

Yours,

R.A.S.

Here is an e-mail that was an absolute certainty to be printed... and it was:

Those that have read my letters in the Herald over the last twenty years probably know that I am a fault-finder by nature, extremely "green" in my outlook and a fierce critic of our local MP and Tamworth Borough Council.

However, I have to concede that Tamworth Borough Council do get some things right.

Every year they present us with a superb floral display in and around our town centre and in the castle grounds, and I am grateful to the ground workers and others that are behind this visual treat.

Periodically the council also provide entertainment for their citizens.

Last summer I was more than happy to attend a pop concert in the castle grounds in which we were treated to great performances from well-known artists and I applaud all those that were involved in the logistics behind this undertaking.

Finally I am also grateful that our household waste is still being collected on a regular basis unlike the disgraceful occurrences that we were witness to in Edinburgh and Coventry during the summer.

Yours,

R.A.S.

Another e-mail sent to everyone without any sort of a reply:

Here we go again into yet another COP meeting; this time at Sharm El Sheikh, and I have to say that I agree with Greta Thunberg that the whole exercise is a complete waste of time.

Why these meetings cannot take place over video phone links rather than pumping yet more CO_2 into the atmosphere from all the delegates' journeys to and from these venues is beyond me!

However, above all of this trivia is the real issue and that is of the impending death of our planet.

It is a 99.9% certainty because democracies cannot face up to the elephant in the room... that of the curtailing of individual freedom!

Unless we legally restrict people's freedom to make unnecessary journeys by car and air we will never get out of the hole we are in... and we all know that this is NEVER going to happen...hence my total and complete scepticism about the fate of our planet!

I'm not terribly sure that I can remember what actually triggered this locally sent e-mail:

Here is a copy of a letter that I sent to the Tamworth Herald many years ago that I recall was NOT printed:

Golf Course Outrage.

There's not a day that goes by when, on watching the television or listening to the radio, one of the major party leaders isn't banging on about transparency in government. Clearly this message hasn't filtered down to the members of Tamworth Borough Council headed by Daniel Cook, who choose to do their dealings behind closed doors! Yes, a meeting to discuss the sale of OUR golf course reportedly took place in complete SECRECY last Thursday!

This is the golf course, I was reminded by one of the Herald's readers last week, that was bequeathed to the council by the NCB for recreational use for a period of fifty years; and that the council have been waiting, vulture-like, for the expiry date to elapse so they can make a few bob...and what better way of making loads of money than by stuffing it full of (unrequired) houses, and never mind the increased risk of flooding to property and land further "downstream", after all, IT'S LOADS O' MONEY!...and who are going to be the possible beneficiaries of some of this loot? Well, can you believe, "specialist sales and marketing agents"!

From green fields, reed buntings, harvest mice, voles, hedgehogs to "specialist sales and marketing agents"...doesn't it make you sick!

R.A.S.

Here is a locally sent e-mail that was printed in the Herald albeit severely edited:

Restricting the movement of peoples is the ONLY way that we can solve the problem of Global Warming.

At the moment the movement of peoples around the world is increasing at a ridiculous rate; on the latest figures there are between 15,500 and 17,500 planes in the air at any one time, of which 10,000 to 12,000 are passenger carriers. This means that over 1,250,000 people are in the air at every minute of every day!

You can imagine how much fuel is required to keep these planes airborne and how much CO_2 is being generated in the process.

On the ground anyone can see how many more vehicles there are on our roads and motorways compared with the days of my youth in the fifties and sixties just by looking at old film footage...the growth is exponential along, of course, with the CO_2 emissions!

Not only are there a ridiculous number of vehicles but the size of these heaps of metal have increased, everyone wants to drive a "gas-guzzler".

What drives this insanity?

Well a lot of it has got to do with the desire of individuals to be "great" at something!

Every day we are inventing new games or pastimes or expanding the old established ones so that someone's little darling can be a world champion!

How long before we have an underwater tiddly-winks world championship or a pogo stick cross-country world-wide tournament?...and, naturally, we now have to have the female equivalent as well!

The run-up to any world-wide championship event means preliminary tournaments across the world or within a country before we get to the actual final itself.

When I was a young man we had no horse racing on a Sunday, one race meeting a day during the week (except possibly two on a Wednesday afternoon) and, joy unbounded, three meetings on a Saturday.

Now we have four or five meetings every day and even two or three on a Sunday! When you consider the movement of people (and horses) to and from these meetings now, you can understand the increase in CO_2 emissions in this small area alone. Much of this expansion of the racing industry is down to the gambling aspect of the sport.

Now take our national game, football, in my youth we had one European competition played by a few of the top teams; we now have THREE major European tournaments contested by up to six clubs from every single country in Europe. All of these competitions are run on a preliminary mini-league format in which all teams play each other home and away.

The number of "fan" movements associated with all of these matches is staggering and must contribute to a significant release of CO_2 into the atmosphere.

Now we are also about to get the female equivalent!

Once again, at the back of all of this is the driving force of the gambling industry.

Please note that this exponential increase in football fixtures is not confined to Europe but is occurring all over the world.

All other sports and pastimes are all following a similar pattern and I suspect that the vast majority of the 1,250,000 people in the air at this moment are engaged in participating or following one sport or pastime or another ...along with many millions of motorists on the ground.

NONE of these movements are necessary compared with the fate of our dying planet!

Yours,

R.A.S.

Here are a couple of recent e-mails that were sent to the Herald but not printed:

There are two issues in the news at the moment that seem to be generating a lot of interest. The first is the location of this year's football World Cup and the politics around this particular location, and the second concerns COP compensation for poor countries affected by global warming.

As regards Qatar getting this year's World Cup final, my personal view on this subject is that the decision to play the final in Qatar was appalling. It was totally unsuitable in many respects and was arrived at by, I suspect, a series of "brown envelope" manoeuvres.

The present Fifa president suggests that the West is full of hypocrisy when it highlights Qatar's record on human rights and he possibly has a point, but what he fails to discuss and does NOT highlight is the CO_2 emissions associated with the holding of this final in Qatar in the first place.

A professor from Lancaster University on Radio 4 this morning suggested that holding the final in Qatar had a very high impact on CO_2 emissions; FIVE TIMES greater than the final held in Russia!

My philosophy about the abuse of human rights in other countries is that we should preach about these things only when we are totally sure that our own house is in order!

Now, as far as COP struggling over compensation sums for those poor countries affected by Global Warming; as much as I sympathise with these countries and their right to such compensation, the movement of money is not going to alter what is going to happen to us all if we do not curb our CO_2 emissions WORLDWIDE!

COP meetings, in their present form, are a complete and utter waste of time as far as I am concerned, but if we are going to continue with them their efforts should be SOLELY involved in reducing CO_2 emissions and nothing else!

Yours,

R.A.S.

And here is the second effort that the Herald did not print:

We all have our own personal stories about being victimised and "put upon" by others, but it is how we react to such occurrences that defines us as individuals.

Many hold their experiences in early life to form (or be associated with) groups of people who have been affected in similar ways to their own, and make the rest of society take note of their particular "grouse" and as a result many have become famous personalities in their own right and rewarded as such!

I was victimised in my youth for being a "grammar-grub" on a council estate.

I had a knife waved in front of my face in Sutton Park by an elder boy for being a "grammar-grub", and on another occasion was beaten up and left in a gutter by another elder boy for the same reason.

However, in later life, I did NOT form a group "Council Grammar School Boys Against Society" and capitalise on my misfortune like so many victimised, and now prominent people in our society, seem to have done!

I JUST BIT THE BULLET AND GOT ON WITH LIFE!

Yours,

R.A.S.

Now, finally, a couple of recent e-mails that were printed in the Herald. This first one was slightly edited:

Because I'm a Friend of Warwickshire Moor I am continually confronted by litter on our site.

I thought I had an excellent idea for tackling this world-wide problem and attempted to introduce my idea to the Earthshot Project.

It was totally impossible...there is NO way that the ordinary person in the street can get their ideas aired in this forum, despite what some members of royalty seem to think!

I made an attempt to get the supermarket Aldi involved but they suggested the idea needed to go to the Earthshot Project...oh yeah!

I am beginning to think that the Earthshot Project is run by a group of elitest and cliquey people that view the project as a way to travel the world and ingratiate themselves with royalty!

If the Earthshot Project had a user-friendly website where your ideas could be seriously scrutinised (and rejected if necessary), instead of one that is just full of self-congratulation, we might be getting somewhere on the way to solving some of the planet's many problems!

Yours,

Ron S.

This second e-mail was printed without alteration:

When I was a young boy I used to play around the gorse bushes in Sutton Park amidst flocks of YELLOWhammer...now all GONE.

Years later I occasionally travelled, by train, to and from my RAF bases in the East Midlands, and out of the train window I often saw fields full of WHITE and BLACK Lapwing...now all GONE.

Twenty-five years ago my partner and I moved to Bolehall and our garden was full of GREENfinch ...now all GONE.

We also had occasional visits by the colourful Bullfinch, flocks of Long-tailed tit and a lesser spotted woodpecker...now all GONE.

This winter for the first time since we have been in our house we have not had a regular friendly visit to our bird table from a RED Robin...where's he GONE?

What sort of colourless world are we bringing our grandchildren up in?

Oh sorry!, silly me, they have, of course, TONS and TONS of bright, shiny colourful bits of PLASTIC they can play with and, no doubt, admire!

Yours,

Ron S.

Finally, this whole story has been about how a single finger tapping on a keyboard can have repercussions in the outside world which may be just local, but could in the right circumstances, possibly, affect the course of how an entire country is run and by whom.

Printed in Great Britain
by Amazon